Things and Things I Need

by Kelly Gaffney

I like my green shoes.

The green shoes look good.

I **want** the green shoes.

3

It is raining.

Look at the water.

It is too wet for the green shoes.

I **need** my boots.

Look at the sun.

It is fun to play.

I **want** to play in the sun.

Here comes Dad.

I will not play in the sun.

I **need** to help my dad.

Look!

I see a little red cake.

It looks good to eat.

I **want** to eat the little red cake.

Here comes Mum.

I cannot eat the little red cake.

I **need** to eat my dinner.

I am in bed.

Look at my book.

I **want** to read my book.

Here comes Dad.

I cannot read my book.

I **need** to go to sleep.